# REBECCA L. BINDER

CONTEMPORARY
WORLD
ARCHITECTS

# REBECCA L. BINDER

Preface by
Stanley Tigerman

Introduction and Text by
Eleanor Lynn Nesmith

Concept and Design by
Lucas H. Guerra
Oscar Riera Ojeda

ROCKPORT
PUBLISHERS

ROCKPORT PUBLISHERS
ROCKPORT, MASSACHUSETTS

First published in the United States of America by:
Rockport Publishers, Inc.
146 Granite Street
Rockport, Massachusetts 01966
Telephone: (508) 546-9590
Fax: (508) 546-7141

Distributed to the book trade and art trade in the U.S. by:
The A.I.A. Press
1735 New York Avenue
Washington, DC 20006
Telephone: 800-365-ARCH
Fax: 800-678-7102

Other distribution by:
Rockport Publishers, Inc.
Rockport, Massachusetts 01966

ISBN 1-56496-151-6

10  9  8  7  6  5  4  3

Editor: Shawna Mullen
Graphic Design: Lucas H. Guerra / Oscar Riera Ojeda
Connexus Visual Communication / Boston
Cover Photo: Visual Arts Facility, University of California, San Diego
©Jeff Goldberg / Esto

Printed in Hong Kong by Regent Publishing Services Limited

# CONTENTS

# Preface

BY STANLEY TIGERMAN

Young (43), a member of a minority (woman) in her profession, an exile from her birthplace (New Jersey), Rebecca L. Binder represents the new breed of architect trained in the United States after World War II. The old ways of measuring architects are no longer particularly applicable to her gender, or generation, or for that matter—to any of the inhabitants of a profession now so dramatically in flux.

In any case, too much is made of the use of analogy as a way of categorizing architects; it puts them in their place too firmly for comfort. Some would say that Ms. Binder's architectural production owes considerable debt to a particular precursor (Frank O. Gehry)—but then so does the work of Eric Owen Moss, Franklin Israel, and a host of consequential others too lengthy to mention. Even Frank Gehry's recent work has itself become self-referential, the power of (his) signature architecture is so alarmingly pervasive.

For our purposes, let's pretend that Mr. Gehry's architecture never existed, in order to see if Ms. Binder's work can sustain scrutiny on an absolute, rather than on a referential/relative basis. Even then, referentiality is difficult to dismiss: from connoisseurship through context, it is vaguely impossible to analyze artistic production intrinsically. In other words, when her production is removed from (its) place, are there characteristics implicit in what she does (and who she is) that are persuasive in and of themselves? So as to remove any suspense, I for one, certainly think so.

East Coast (read NY) architects are too near, and thus too influenced by European linkages to be free from analogous interpretation: after all, all that Eurodrivel lands first on America's Ellis (read Manhattan) Island. The intellectual pretentiousness—common to NYARCH (mis)readings—owe an obvious debt (by dint of proximity) to that place from which so many of us spring as to manifest our collective insecurities in the architectural rationalization process so common to the jury system extant in architectural educational institutions throughout the land.

Because I am a native of America's heartland, I thought that we were free of such linkages, and that our work could be fairly judged on absolute terms: wrong, as usual! As NY looks East for validation, so do we in the midwest also look to the rising sun for approbation from our Eastern counterparts. Thus, we hold ourselves hostage to relativism at all levels. Only our Western frontier generally, and LA'S "dream machine" specifically, seems to have escaped this fate, suggesting a sub-consciously Jungian potentiality

to address an architecture by someone like Ms. Binder.

There is a kind of verisimilitude—a certainty—to Ms. Binder's production that is made manifest by her immensely diverse, ever-growing practice that, in just over 15 years has caused a large number of institutional and commercial work to come about (in addition to the expected domestic work engaged in by most fledgling practices) all of which has preserved the immediacy implicit in what she does. In other words, the dangers of the shift of scale from small to large seems to have had little impact on the freshness of all that she puts her pencil to. From the earliest moments in her smallest houses—built and unbuilt alike—her architecture has exhibited an effervescence that is simply more than the place in which it is situated: and it is never, ever executed with an uncertain hand. It is that sureness, that deft way of courageously connecting forms—and materials—that characterizes what she does as a kind of unique signature.

To adventure far afield is certainly one of the great joys of architecture, and Ms. Binder's buildings exhibit nothing if not adventuresomeness. Complex far beyond something as droll as "program," resisting "readability," Ms. Binder's buildings defy easy categorization (despite her drawing methods that show all the parts of the whole), which is why the "analogy" method is not particularly useful here to explicate her process. The one linkage that does stand out is the autobiographical one.

While there is some truth to the fact that all architects are, in some ways, autobiographically inclined, Ms. Binder AND her buildings are clearly cut from the same cloth: so clearly intertwined, in fact, as to make them in all ways indistinguishable. Bold, even brash, ambitious, NEVER saccharine, Ms. Binder AND her architecture are ultimately unforgettable. Often unexpected, yet always driven solidly home, Ms. Binder's arguments AND her architecture tell us that this discipline of ours is no longer the purview of musty aristocracy alone...this is a new day when architects can just damn well stand up and argue their case vociferously without the fear of being put down because of their brashness. The "little boy with the curl in the middle of his forehead" is dead; long live the curl in the middle of her forehead. Because of Ms. Binder and others like her, generationally AND gender alike, this is now a land for which it is de rigeur to resist middle age. Clearly Ms. Binder AND her architecture are in no way going through a "crise a quarante ans." And that, in and of itself, is exciting.

# Introduction

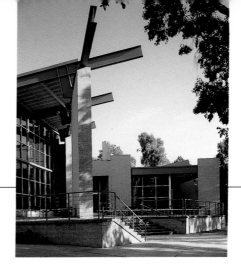

Southern California with its energetic economy and wide open spaces has long been a land of opportunity and a fertile proving ground for architects. A freedom from tradition and conformity has characterized its architecture throughout the 20th century. Within this environment, Rebecca L. Binder has assembled an impressive body of work beginning more than a decade ago with the completion of the four-unit, Pacific Townhouse condominium, winner of a National AIA Honor Award in 1985. Over the years, her practice has grown to include a partner, Kim Walsh, and has expanded beyond residential work to commercial and public buildings, including a fire station, an airport terminal, and a variety of academic buildings.

Binder acknowledges a deep respect for strong, simple, and pragmatic Modernist precedents and views her work as an evolution of Modernism. Although a kinship can be drawn between Binder's approach to design and that of other contemporary Southern California practitioners, from Frank Gehry to Morphosis to Eric Owen Moss, she possesses the kind of confident understanding that allows an architect to forge dynamic spatial arrangements that reflect her own idiom.

The strong composition evident in this work serves more than merely aesthetic ends. The visual energy of

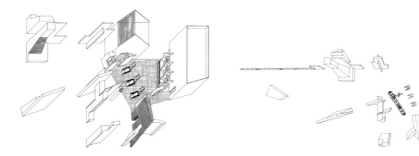

these buildings results, in part, from creative responses to pragmetic issues. The arrangement of discrete parts sometimes resolves challenges of the site, as with the Garner Residence. The programmatic requirements for the Visual Arts Facility (at the University of California, San Diego) resulted in open hallways, courtyards, and open-air work spaces for artists.

In as much as Binder interprets every commission based on a careful evaluation of the program, she remains committed to an evolution of design and affirms the critical importance of collaboration. She credits ongoing creative interchange with Kim Walsh, teamwork of the talented and dedicated staff, and an extensive interaction with clients. Rather than setting out to capture design opportunities, Binder takes her cues from the building program itself. Sometimes opportunities arise from coincidences. Unusual spaces and unexpected scenes are created as new spatial relationships emerge.

While these designs create a physical presence through mass and volume, the buildings are equally characterized by a use of materials that articulates a studied response to site and surroundings. Even the earliest projects draw from a palette of common building materials—concrete block, stucco, metal, and wood. As the work has grown,

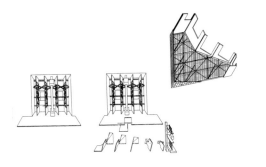

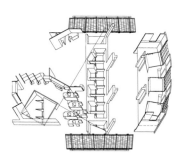

the use of these everyday materials has become increasingly refined. Although richly finished woods, steel, cast-in-place concrete, and stone are finding places in her work, it is the lowly, industrial materials that still give Binder's buildings their tough and characteristic grain.

Binder aligns with a tradition of Modernism but instills her buildings with a sense of spatial complexity and experiential intrigue. Eschewing formalistic design, the work in these pages is crafted to fit the program and to reflect the operational character as well as the respective context.

—Eleanor Lynn Nesmith
Birmingham, Alabama

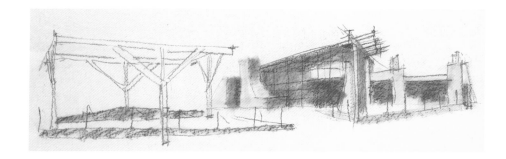

The confident use of common materials and an adroit combination of forms give these buildings a unique signature. From top to bottom: Information Computer Sciences/Engineering Research Facility III; Fischer Residence; Visual Arts Facility.

Works ▶

# University Dining Complex

CALIFORNIA POLYTECHNIC STATE UNIVERSITY, SAN LUIS OBISPO
SAN LUIS OBISPO, CALIFORNIA

An expansion and major renovation transformed an institutional 1950s food service building into a lively dining complex and campus gathering spot, consisting of a 500-seat university dining room, a 400-seat snack bar, and a pre-function space for campus conferences and social events. The original 20,000-square-foot food facility was generally featureless. To give the building increased visibility along the street and to provide daylight, the renovation literally broke out of the box of the original single-story structure.

The architect carved out a new circulation path through the facility. A pair of raised lightwells, with gable-ended skylights of glass, flood the dining hall with natural light. An expressed structural system, part of both the original and the remodeled building, supports the roof additions and opens up interior spaces. Adjacent to the renovated formal dining room, a new patio enclosure functions as an "outdoor room." With its three operable garage doors, this pavilion doubles as a protected area for students to queue for the meal ticket window and provides a space for university and conference functions. The pavilion's roof and clerestory return are totally clad in translucent sandwich panels. New entrance canopies, also constructed of translucent sandwich panels with steel structural supports, enliven the north and south facades of the snack bar.

A third new skylight crowns the expanded snack bar serving area. To accommodate additional seating in the snack bar, the architect incorporated a series of "storefront" dining niches. The east wall, which also incorporates three glazed garage doors and the brick material of the original 50s facade, has been pushed out to create a long, narrow enclosure within a curving facade.

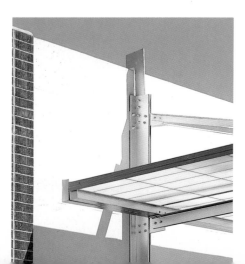

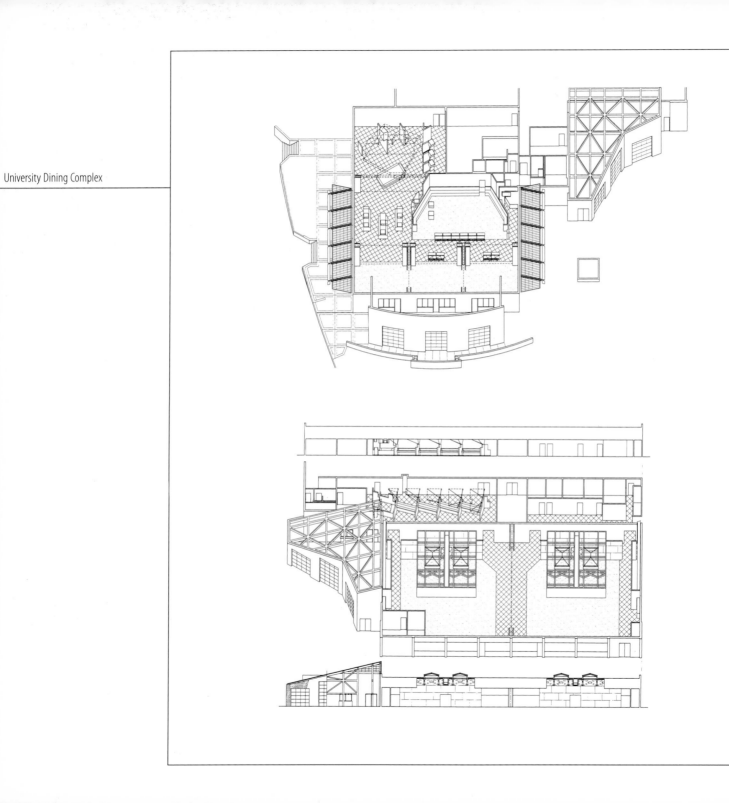

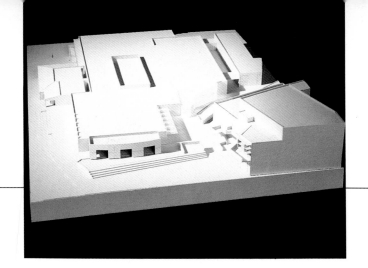

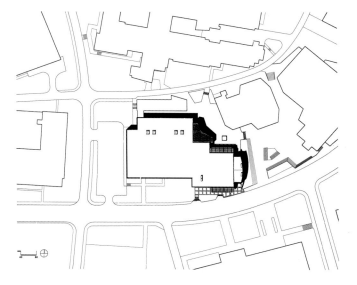

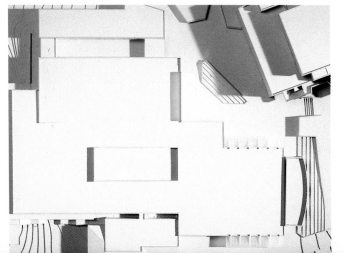

The expanded California Polytechnic State University Dining Complex is arranged to create a stronger presence on the campus (middle). The single-story facility is organized into three main spaces—a central dining room for students on the meal plan, an informal snack bar (opposite page), and a new pre-function space.

The architect opened the dining complex with an intricate, exposed structural system of columns, beams, and trusses. Roofs, clerestories, and skylights clad in translucent sandwich panels and glass provide natural daylight. The University dining room's serving area features custom-made cafeteria fixtures, exposed steel ceiling supports, and a patterned floor to create a lively dining environment.

# Visual Arts Facility

The first building in the University of California, San Diego's Fifth College, the Visual Arts Facility is located on a pivotal, four-acre site between existing academic buildings, the new campus's center to the west, and an untamed canyon to the east. The new 71,500-square-foot arts complex creates a bold presence in the evolving campus landscape.

The program called for private faculty offices, individual studios for students and professors, and adjacent work yards. Given the warm Southern California climate and these strict programmatic requirements, the architect organized the facility as five discrete structures in a village-like assemblage connected by courtyards and open-air walkways. While each component assumes a unique form and character—according to its function—the ensemble is a coherent micro-campus with an underlying adherence to Modernist tradition.

The facades of the three freestanding buildings of the complex are connected by various gates and screens to offer programmatically required privacy, and to create a continuous border along the west elevation fronting Russell Drive. An assertive, columned portal with a curving, metal-clad canopy marks the center's formal campus front entrance, while a second major public access opens to the south with an intimate plaza leading into an open-air lobby. The overall plan of the Visual Arts Facility is organized in a loose interpretation of a tartan grid.

A two-story structure at the heart of the complex is capped with symmetrical bowed roofs. It

contains photography and computer laboratories, media viewing rooms, and 51 graduate student studios. Anchoring the northern corner of the site, a shed-like building accommodates wood, metal, and framing workshops. The most formally articulated volume of the ensemble houses the most public functions of the facility—a "black-box" performance space, a public exhibition gallery, and a seminar room.

Visual Arts Facility

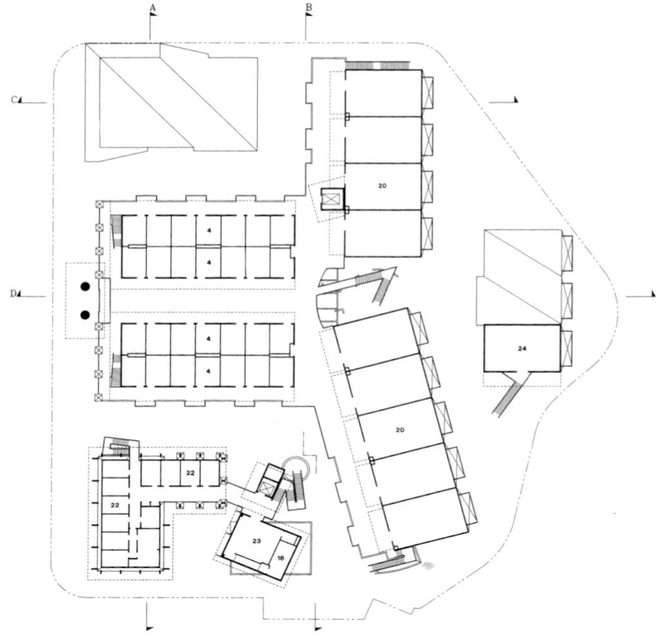

1   METAL SHOP
2   WOOD SHOP
3   FRAMING SHOP
4   GRADUATES
5   PHOTOGRAPHY LAB
6   STUDIO
7   MEDIA VIEWING
8   LOCKER
9   DARKROOM
10  WORK AREA
11  COMPUTING ARTS LAB
12  ELECTRONICS LAB
13  EDITING LAB
14  RESTROOM
15  ASSEMBLY PERFORMANCE
16  CONTROL ROOM
17  LOBBY
18  EXHIBIT/GALLERY
19  COMMONS
20  FACULTY STUDIO
21  ELECTRICAL SUBSTATION
22  FACULTY OFFICE
23  SEMINAR ROOM
24  VISITING FACULTY STUDIO

SECOND FLOOR PLAN

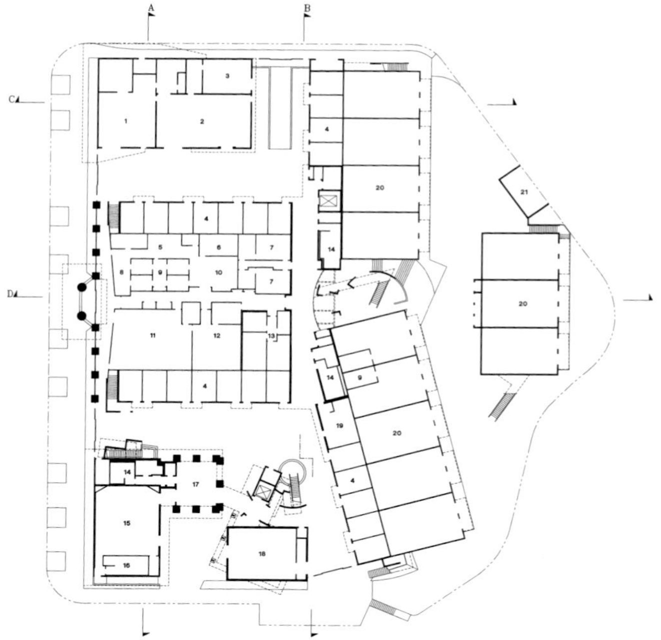

FIRST FLOOR PLAN

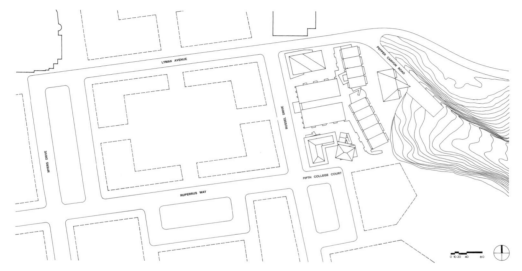

The Visual Arts Facility lies on a pivotal site between the existing university campus to the west and north, and a natural canyon to the east. The architectural design organizes the facility into a series of five buildings, with open courtyards between to provide outdoor studio work spaces.

PEPPER CANYON ELEVATION

SECTION B

The clustered configuration of the Visual Arts Facility creates a series of open spaces, conjuring the image of an Italian hillside village. A black-box performance space anchors the southwest corner of the facility (opposite page). A series of steel doors links the theater with an intimate entrance courtyard (top).

Visual Arts Facility

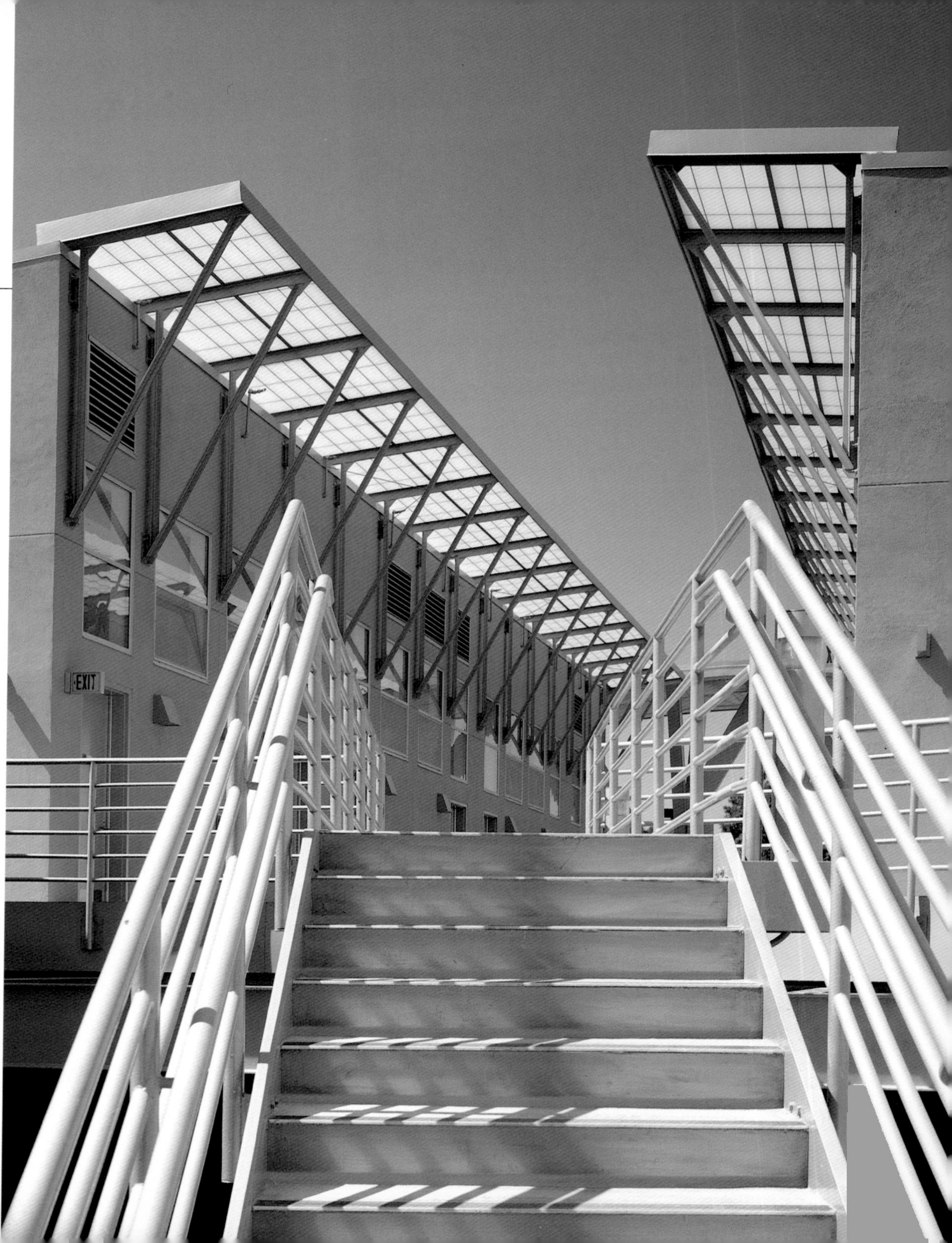

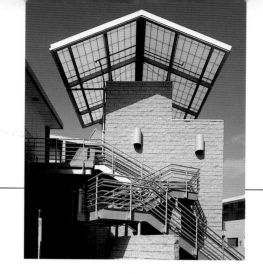

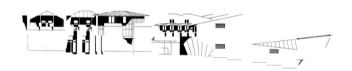

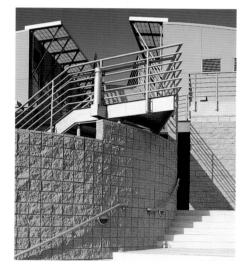

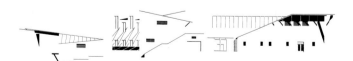

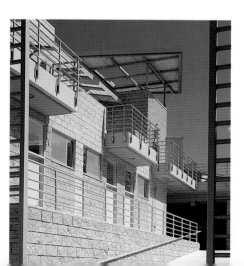

A second-floor promenade between blocks of student studios has continuous canopies (opposite page). These steel-framed sunshades are roofed in translucent sandwich panels, and the translucent roof of an elevator tower to the seminar room echoes the screening canopy material (top). The balconies of the graduate student studio block feature painted steel pipe rails (bottom).

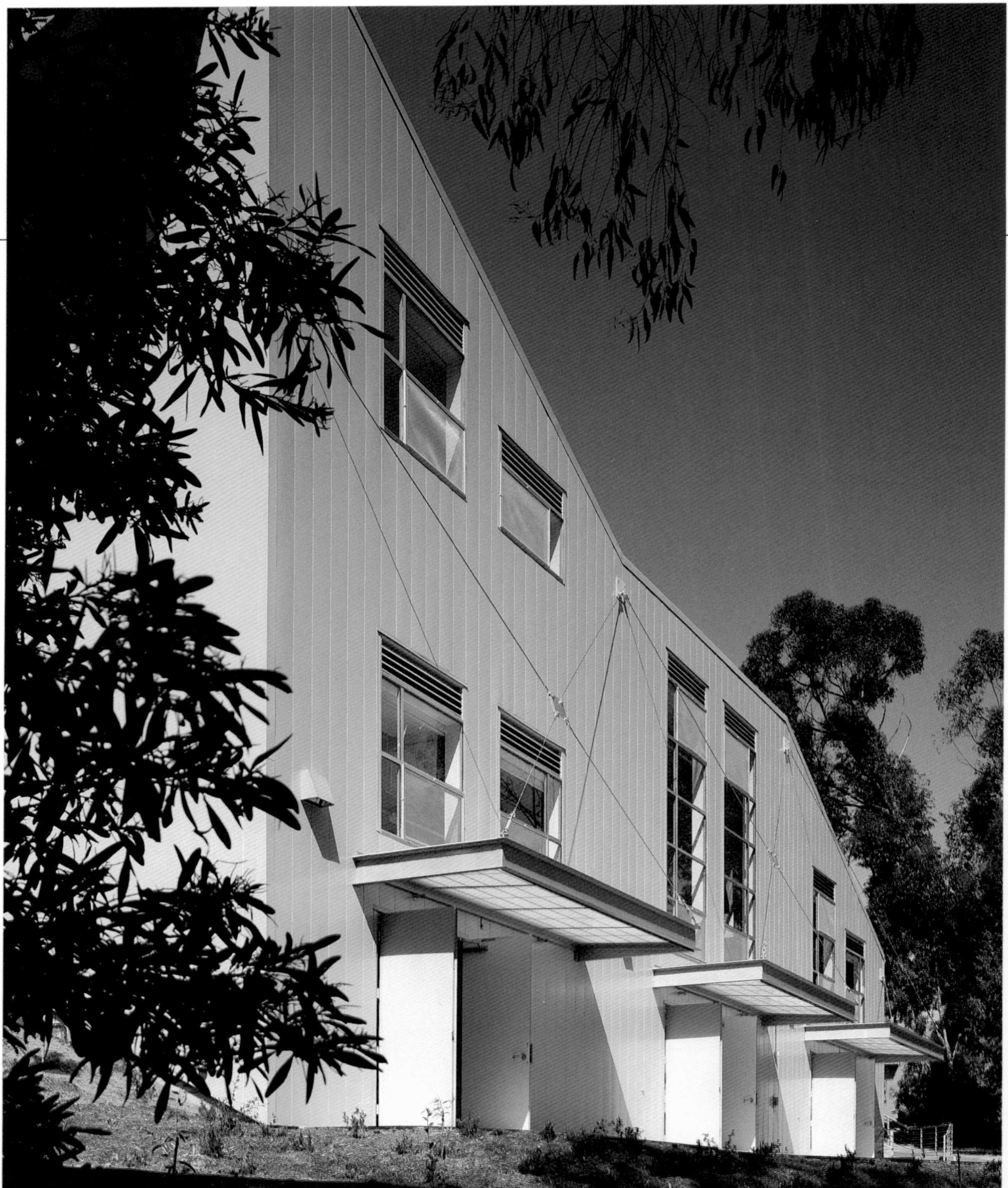

The building's palette of materials includes split-faced and smooth concrete block, painted steel siding, natural wood, and painted steel bridges, balconies, and stairways. A hull-shaped screen crafted of cedar encloses a stairway (bottom). Angled studio blocks along the rear of the site give the complex an industrial stance, and form a "town wall" to the canyon (opposite page).

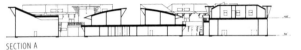

SECTION A

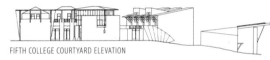

FIFTH COLLEGE COURTYARD ELEVATION

RUSSELL DRIVE ELEVATION

OBLIQUE ELEVATION

Student studios open onto a second-floor court, and frame the view through the facility's assertive entrance portal (top). Large projecting canopies shade the ground floor double doors to the studios (bottom). At night, the large windows and staggered rooflines create a dramatic profile (opposite page).

# Information Computer Sciences/
# Engineering Research Facility Phase III

UNIVERSITY OF CALIFORNIA, IRVINE
IRVINE, CALIFORNIA

Binder's second structure at the University of California, Irvine campus is a 16,000-square-foot academic building that completes the computer/engineering quadrangle designed in two earlier phases by Frank Gehry. The facility has a cross-axial orientation, and is composed of paired, stucco-clad volumes, which offer maximum flexibility for large research bays and small office spaces—without the pretense of universal space.

The three-story ICS/ERF III building is sited to respond to the original ring mall geometry of the campus and to new design guidelines that require the facility to have arcades along the pedestrian path. A three-story wing defines the orthogonally planted olive grove in the Engineering Quad. This volume is articulated with a ceremonial stairway of steel and concrete, defined by four concrete block pillars and a timber canopy announcing the third-floor entrance. To the west is the facility's torqued "tail," a skewed volume clad in a deep blue stucco and roofed with red metal. This wing conforms to the geometry of the arc of the pedestrian ring mall. Along its north and south elevations Binder designed elaborate arcades of heavy timber "trees", supported on concrete block columns, through which to view the building. As a counter point to the grand stairway facing the Engineering Quad, a finely finished, redwood-clad stairway rises along the wing's west facade and is partially screened behind a stucco wall. Without the benefit of grand lobbies, these open stairways and abstract timber arcades provide transition spaces between indoors and out.

Information Computer Sciences/
Engineering Research Facility Phase III

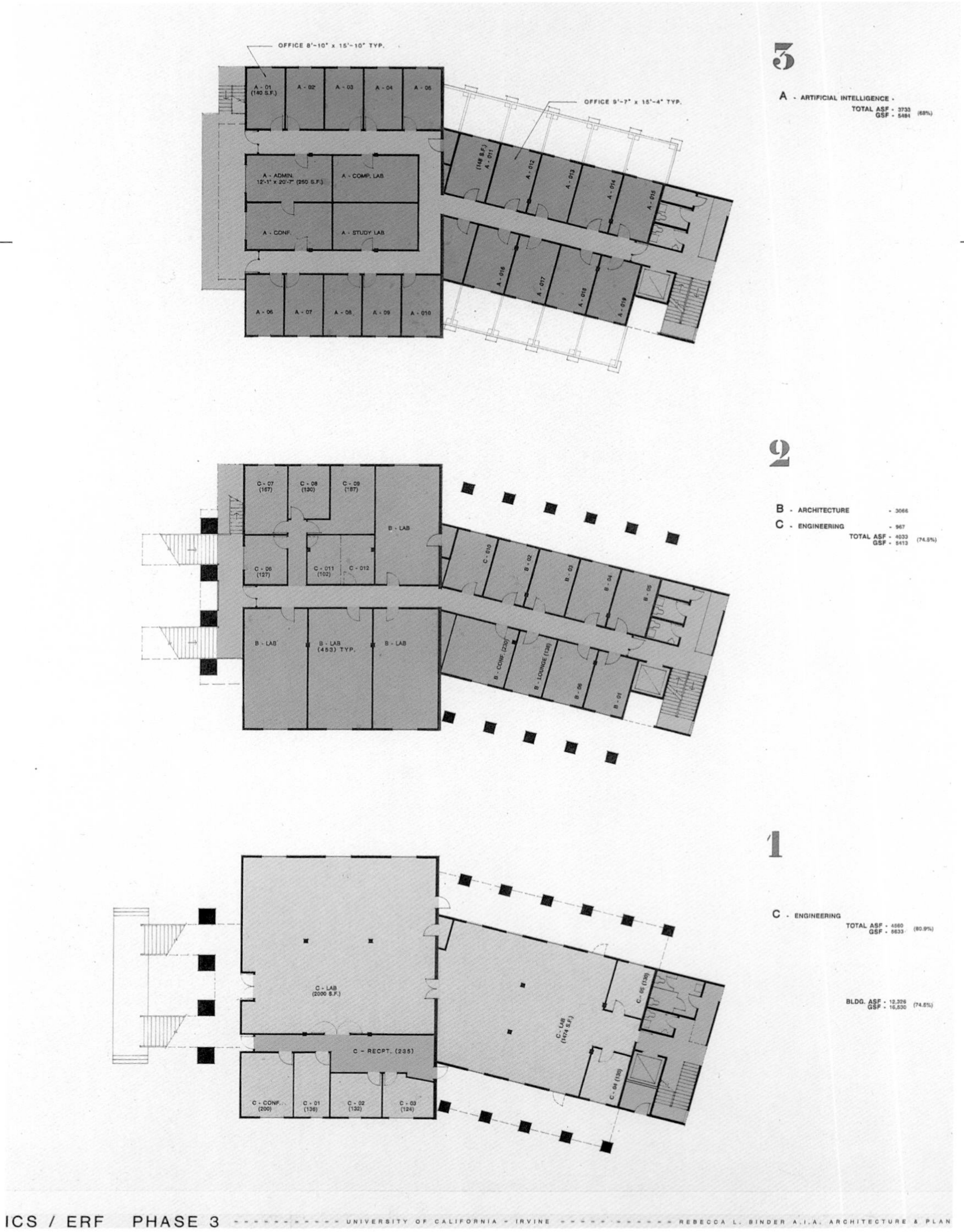

OFFICE 8'-10" x 15'-10" TYP.
OFFICE 9'-7" x 15'-4" TYP.
3
A - ARTIFICIAL INTELLIGENCE -
TOTAL ASF - 3733
GSF - 5484 (68%)
A - ADMIN.
A - COMP. LAB
A - CONF.
A - STUDY LAB
2
B - ARCHITECTURE - 3066
C - ENGINEERING - 967
TOTAL ASF - 4033
GSF - 5413 (74.5%)
B - LAB
B - LAB (453) TYP.
1
C - ENGINEERING
TOTAL ASF - 4560
GSF - 5633 (80.9%)
BLDG. ASF - 12,326
GSF - 16,530 (74.6%)
C - LAB (2000 S.F.)
C - RECPT. (235)
ICS / ERF PHASE 3
UNIVERSITY OF CALIFORNIA - IRVINE
REBECCA L. BINDER A.I.A. ARCHITECTURE & PLAN

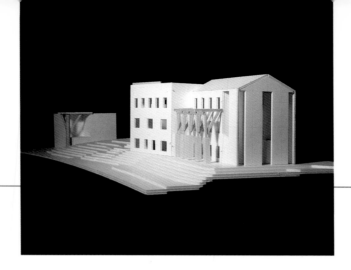

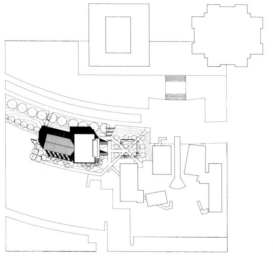

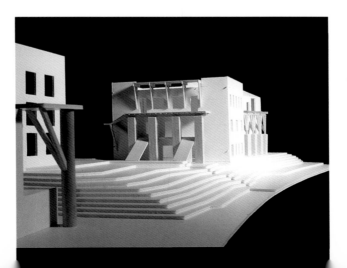

This building, which completes the university's computer sciences/engineering facilities, is sited to respond to the quad's orthogonally planted olive grove and the arc of the pedestrian ring mall on the main campus. The building's cross-axial arrangement of spaces affords flexibility with large bays and small offices (opposite page).

Information Computer Sciences/
Engineering Research Facility Phase III

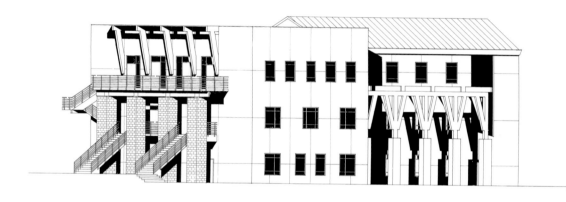

An aerial view of the computer sciences/
engineering quadrangle reveals the
articulated organization of phase III
and its relationship to the original Frank
Gehry structures (top). Facing the quad,
the main entrance is defined by a
ceremonial stairway crafted of steel
(bottom and overleaf).

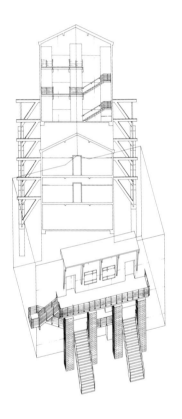

A secondary stairway rises within a protected alcove along the building's west elevation. Arcades composed of heavy timber "trees" define the north and south elevations. The stairway and bold wooden arcades take the place of grand interior lobbies, functioning as a transition between indoors and out.

Information Computer Sciences/
Engineering Research Facility Phase III

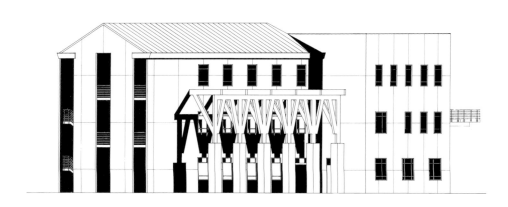

Arcaded facades of the torqued "tail"
of the building respond to the ring
mall geometry of the campus, and
serve as part of the urban scaled *leit-
motif*. The timber arcade presents an
inviting facade along the computer
sciences/engineering quad parking lot
(middle and opposite page).

# Social Sciences Satellite Food Facility

## UNIVERSITY OF CALIFORNIA, IRVINE
## IRVINE, CALIFORNIA

More than 30 years ago, the late William L. Pereira conceived the University of California's Irvine campus as a utopian academic village. In the mid-1980s, the university embarked on a new cycle of construction, commissioning nationally recognized architecture firms and talented young architects to design new projects. Under this building program, Rebecca Binder was hired to design a 5,800-square-foot cafeteria for a prominent site within the perimeter of the university's original, central garden mall.

The result is a crisply articulated angular building that reflects the radial geometry of the original campus master plan. The architect likens the food facility to an archaeological excavation of the campus with its axes etched on the terrain like remnants of the past reinterpreted and its structural members appearing as found objects. The most prominent feature of the facility is an extended roof line of overhanging steel beams, pointing upward and toward the center of the park on a north-south orientation. This sheltered extension creates a partially protected outdoor eating area.

The enclosure walls of the dining hall feature exposed floor-to-roof windows, framed in a grid of anodized aluminum. These glass walls afford views to the park and reveal activity within the building both day and night. All interior furnishings and fixtures are integral parts of the design, including tall freestanding cashier stands that accentuate the verticality of the dining hall. The new food facility is a lively and inviting eatery that mediates between its ponderous, institutional neighbors and its park-like setting.

Social Sciences Satellite Food Facility

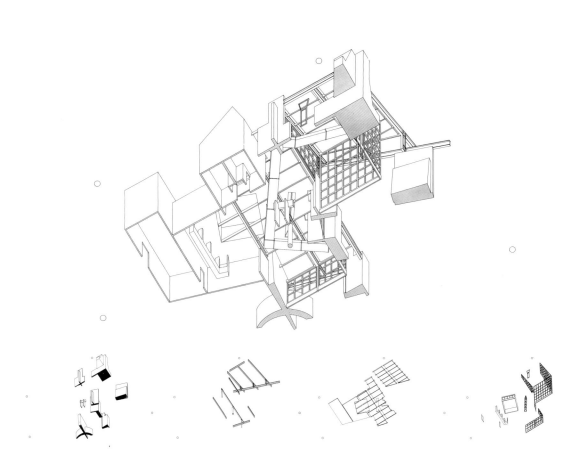

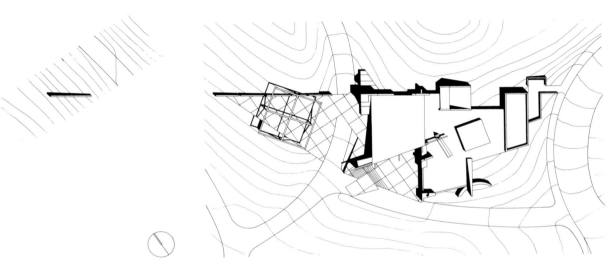

The Satellite Food Facility is located on a prominent site within the original circular mall of the University of California, Irvine. The building is conceived as a series of interconnected structures and positioned to respond to the existing geometries and patterns of the campus master plan.

In the park-like setting of the college's central green, the food facility's outdoor trellis mediates between natural and man-made spaces with its canopy of steel "trees" (top). Both indoor and outdoor seating areas are situated to take advantage of the best views of the park (overleaf).

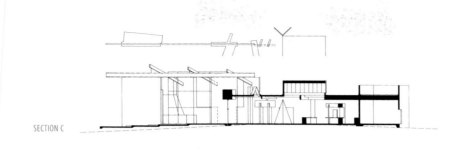

SECTION C

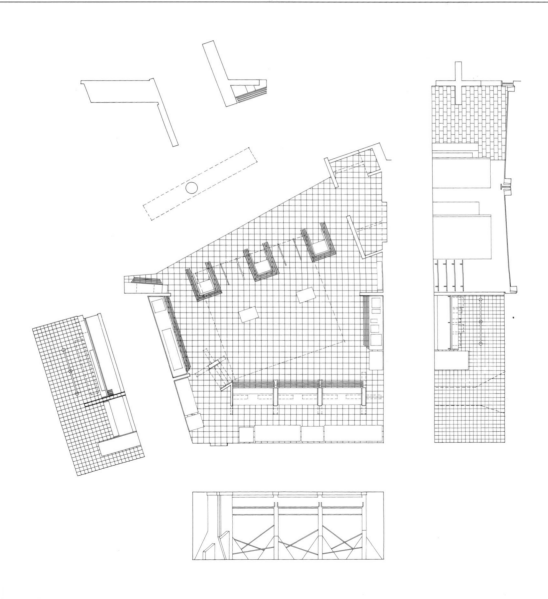

Social Sciences Satellite Food Facility

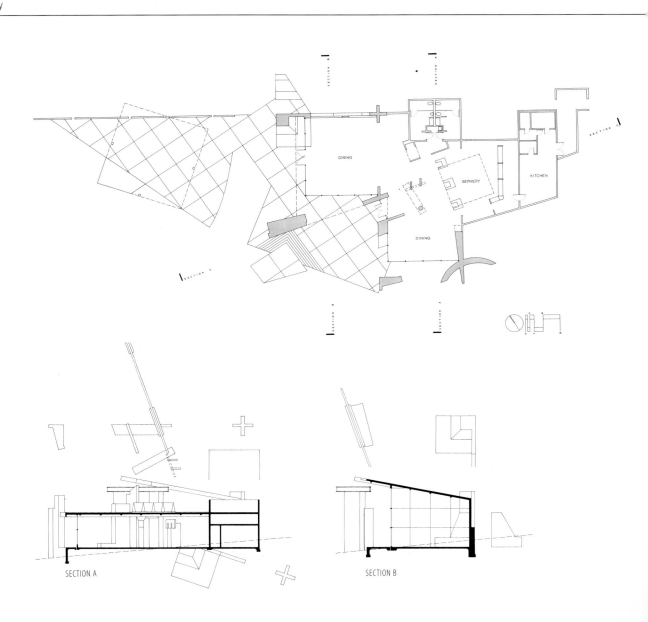

DINING

SERVERY

KITCHEN

DINING

SECTION A

SECTION B

The building's prow-like form creates a light and airy dining area that seats 180 patrons. Clerestories and floor-to-ceiling windows, all framed in a grid of anodized aluminum, open the space to natural light. Exposed structural and mechanical systems combined with custom fixtures and furnishings complement the building's dramatic form.

# Eats Restaurant

EL SEGUNDO, CALIFORNIA

Eats Restaurant is a chic little cafe in a renovated storefront. The original structure was a shoebox-like volume, measuring 12 by 60 feet, with a ceiling height of 12 feet. To create a street presence, Binder carved out a portico perpendicular to the sidewalk and added a colorful canopy. The muted yellow and purple pastels of the exterior stucco finishes are repeated inside for walls, doors, and trim.

To intensify the drama of the interior space, the architect defined the volume with a custom lighting fixture that runs the length of the cafe and is suspended by cables. In the middle of the space, a pair of floating neon strips extend through the cafe, bathing the room in a faintly rosy light. On both walls, sheet metal light-troughs anchor the cable system.

A pale gray, cut-out pie case echoes the shape of the vaguely anthropomorphic exterior facade and shields the bar area from the 30-seat dining area. At the rear, a wall carved to reflect the suspended cable form conceals a kitchen/preparation area.

Eats Restaurant is small with a simple footprint, yet the transverse planes of the facade, the recessed entry, and the articulated pie case mediate the zones of the cafe to create a definite progression from sidewalk to foyer to eating area and bar. The character of this design derives from the architect's consistent application of a few well-thought-out organizing elements, which give this project a stance that exceeds its modest size and budget.

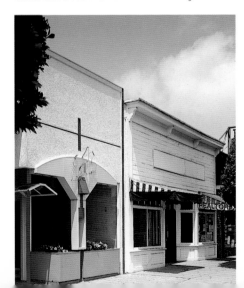

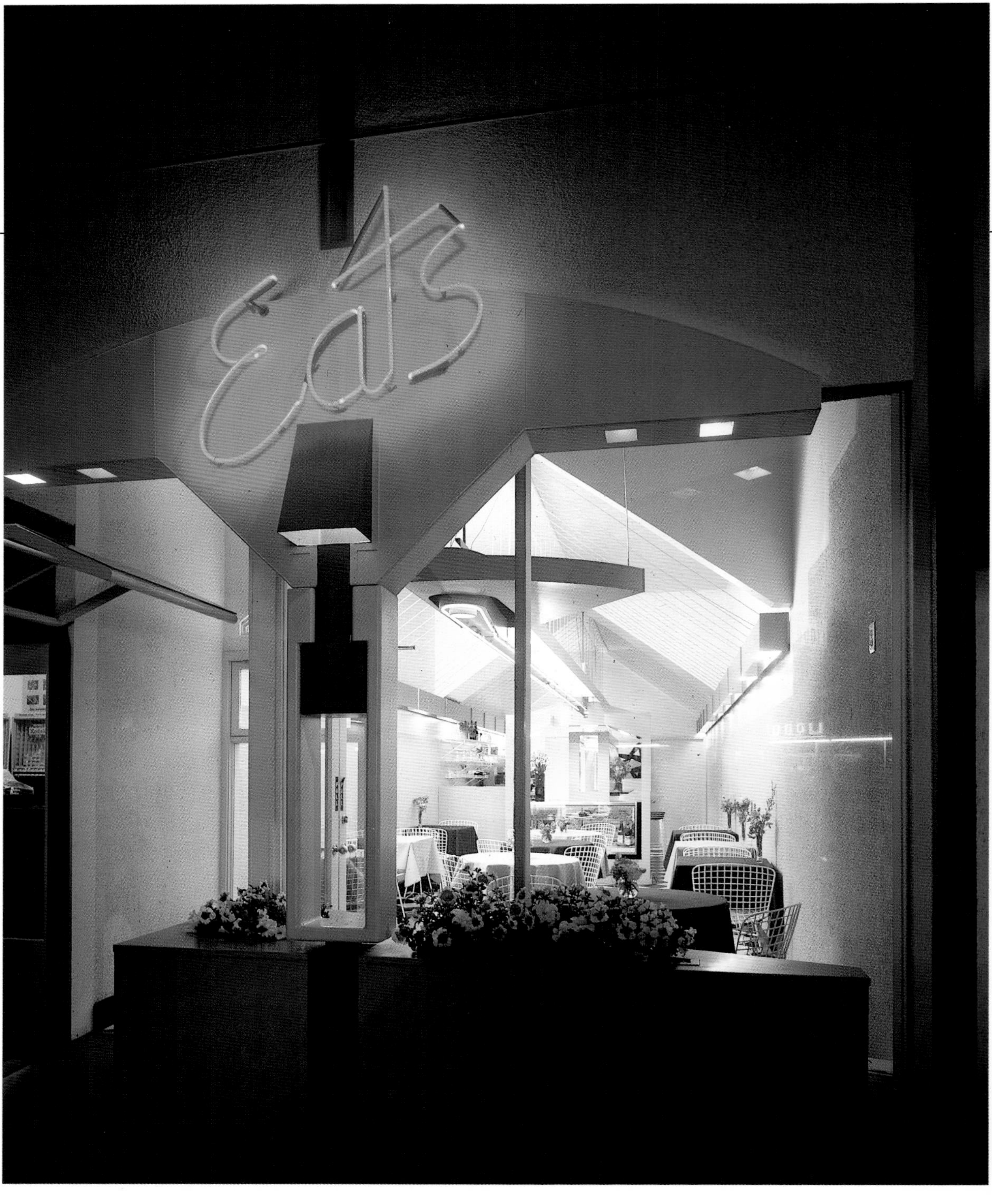
Eats

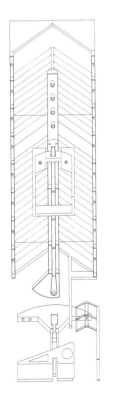

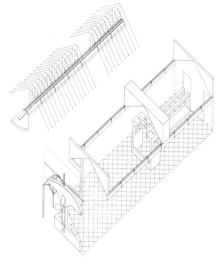

The long narrow footprint of the original structure set the design parameters for this simple eatery (top and bottom). A linear light fixture, suspended by a series of cables, runs the length of the space (top). At night, the exterior neon lighting and dramatic interior illumination create a lively presence on the street (opposite page).

# Pacific Townhouses

SANTA MONICA, CALIFORNIA

An architect's first project often sets the standards for a new practice. When Binder established her own office in 1979, her first project was the four-unit Pacific Townhouses, which proved to be a precursor of buildings to come. The structure exploits abstracted forms and prosaic materials, packing a visual punch into a modest project.

Located less than a block from the Pacific Ocean, the complex is organized as a linear series of four 30-foot cubes oriented to the west. The four units sit on a concrete-block plinth that accommodates semi-subterranean parking.

Configured much like a Chinese wooden puzzle, the exterior of each condominium unit appears as an eroded cube, carved away to reveal the contours of the spaces within. Each townhouse is further articulated with a bright red "X" and an extending steel "arm" that not only adds visual interest but diagrams the transfer of the lateral loads of that facade. Subtle gray stucco walls provide a neutral background for the colorful structural accents, taut railings, and punched windows.

Interior volumes are a pure expression of the exterior forms. At street level, paired steel doors open onto a two-car garage and storage area for each unit. Three bedrooms are located on each unit's second floor, which is accessible either through the garage or through a continuous entrance deck that

runs along the east facade a half-level above grade. The third floor contains the dining room, kitchen, and a double-height living room enlivened with a floor-to-ceiling peaked window. A quarter-vaulted loft with access to the extensive roof decks overlooks the third floor, crowning the building with a soaring space.

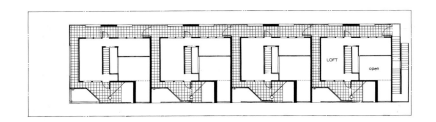

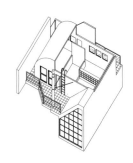

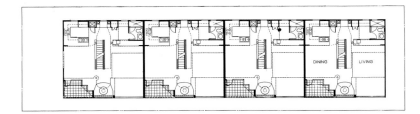

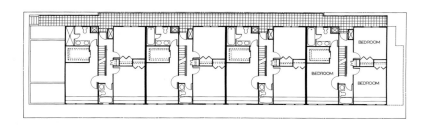

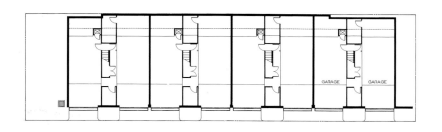

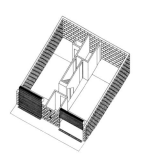

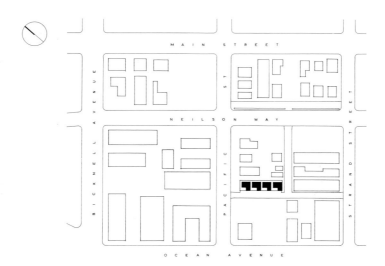

MAIN STREET

BICKNELL AVENUE

MAIN ST

STRAND STREET

NEILSON WAY

PACIFIC

OCEAN AVENUE

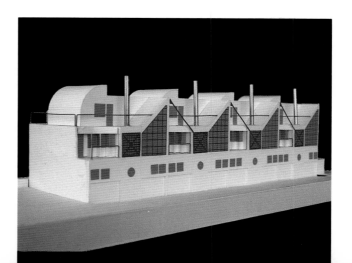

The four-unit Pacific Townhouses are located in a dense urban residential neighborhood in Santa Monica. The longitudinal axis of the site is oriented to the Pacific Ocean, located a block to the west. The design evolved into four autonomous housing units with the living and dining spaces on the upper levels to take advantage of ocean views. Bedrooms are located on the second floor; a double-garage with storage is set at grade.

The east facade of the Townhouses (top and opposite page middle) presents a more private face to adjacent properties, while the west facade (bottom and opposite page bottom) opens to ocean views. The townhouses are set atop a concrete block plinth.

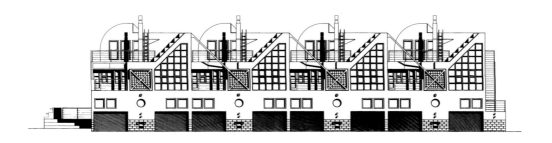

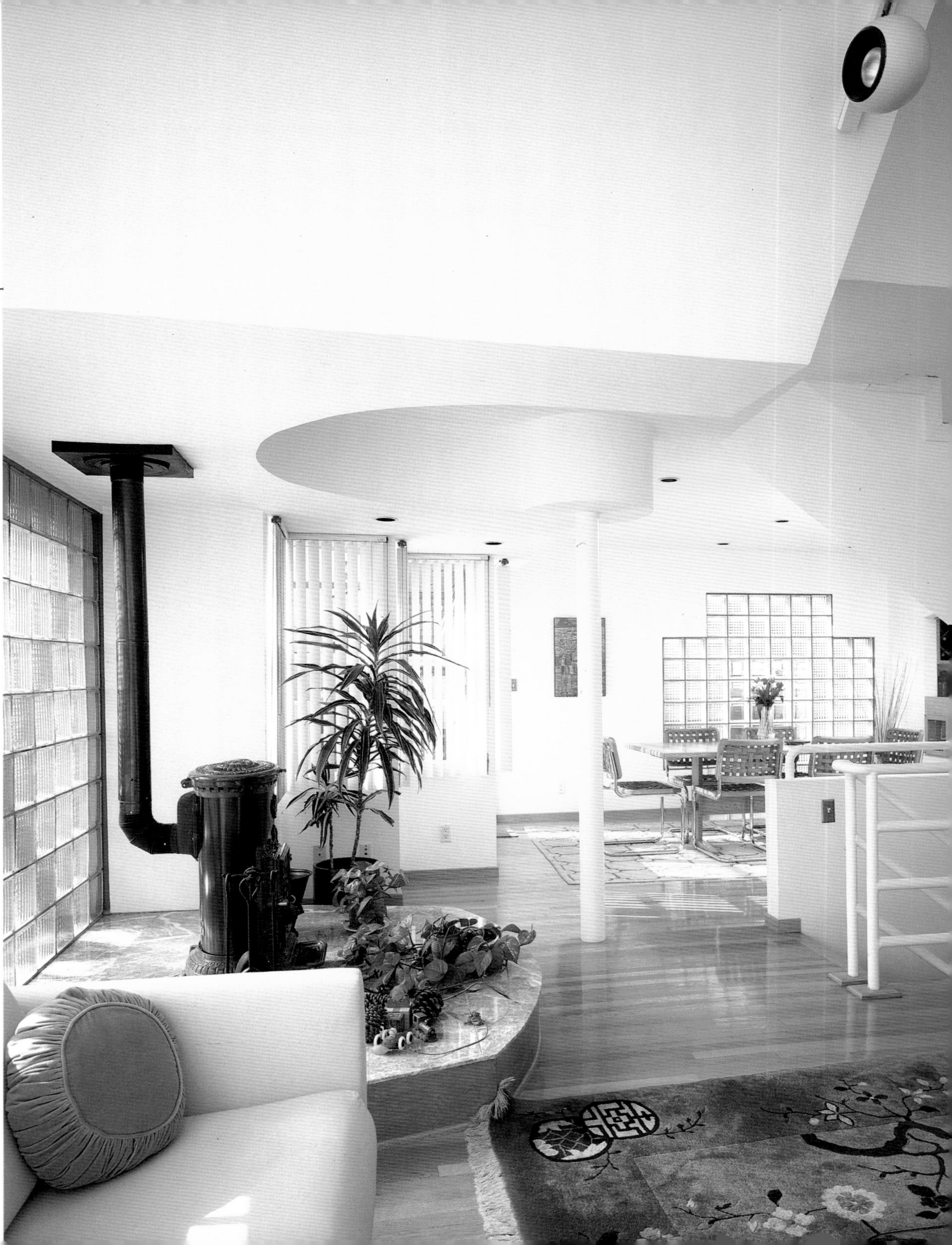

Interiors are designed as open, voluminous spaces. Exposed stairways with painted steel railings create a sense of movement between the four levels of each town-house. A double-height, square-paned window that comes to a peak dominates the main living space.

# Armacost Duplex

This duplex apartment building manages the difficult task of setting a new standard of design while fitting in gracefully with its unpretentious surroundings of postwar stucco houses and apartments that line the block. Binder successfully transforms a simple building type, without creating contrived elaborations or violating its essential ordinariness.

The restrictive 25- by 140-foot site dictated a long, narrow footprint stretching across the property. Thus, the two-unit complex is configured as a pair of 16-foot-wide houses separated by an elevated deck. Each 1,600-square-foot unit features a highly articulated street elevation. The complex is crowned with a split-shed roof and sits atop a concrete-block plinth that encloses a four-car garage. A curving concrete-block wall at grade carves out a small, semi-circular entry courtyard.

Working with a minimal budget of 43 dollars per square foot, Binder chose an inexpensive combination of three-quarter-inch fiberboard siding and stucco cladding for the wood-frame structure, instead of expensive ornamental details. Although the two units are nearly identical, Binder heightened the project's visual impact by alternating the materials on similar elements of each house. Along the Armacost Street elevation, the building's main shed-roofed volume is clad in fiberboard with the decks and stairway finished in stucco, while on the facade facing the alley the corresponding volumes have a reversed combination of a stucco-finished and fiberboard-finished decks and stairways.

Armacost Duplex

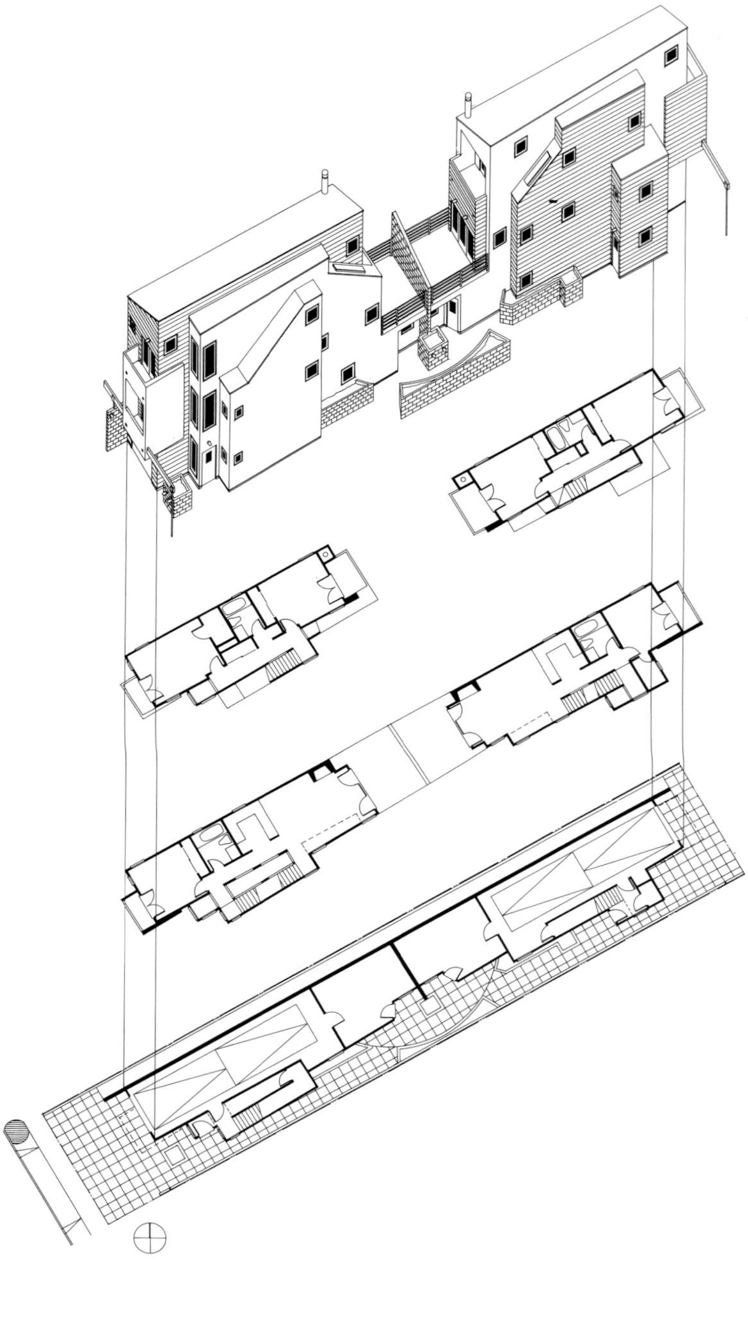

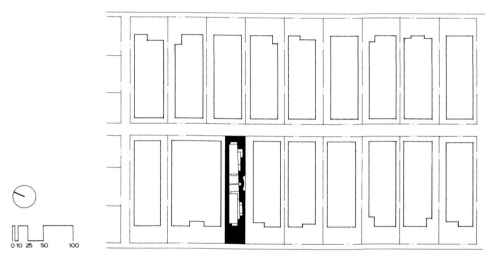

0 10 25  50      100

The Armacost Duplex is located on
a long narrow site—25 feet by 140
feet—in a modest residential neighborhood. The architect organized the two-
unit complex as a pair of 16-foot-wide
houses, each measuring approximately
1,600 square feet. The two-level houses
are each set on a concrete-block plinth
that encloses a two-car garage.

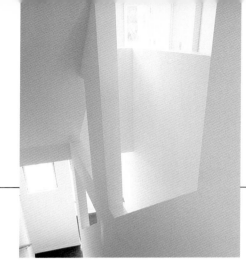

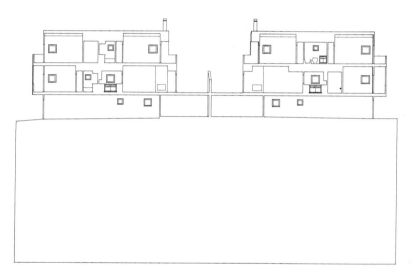

A simple palette of exterior materials, including stucco, fiberboard siding, and a concrete block base, (opposite page) reflects a straightforward esthetic. Both the interior and exterior design eschew ornamental flourishes, relying instead on simple but bold geometric forms. The two units are separated by an elevated deck (middle).

# Fischer Residence

PLAYA DEL REY, CALIFORNIA

The Fischer Residence, like many of Binder's residential designs, is a cluster of related forms that turns a simple building into a sculptural complex. The 3,400-square-foot house appears to break down into three smaller units. The mass is differentiated into gabled volumes and terraced components, which conform to the principal internal events. Color coding characterizes the design parti and creates a sense of proportion. Steel railings and redwood timber balustrades screen second-floor terraces and balconies.

 The house is located on an irregular triangular site at the corner of two streets in a quiet residential neighborhood. Anchoring the eastern boundary of the property is a longitudinal spine containing the family room, kitchen, dining room, guest room, and garage; a square pavilion containing the living room dominates the western corner of the site.

 A glazed foyer traversed by a second-floor studio leads into both the living room and the hall. This long, thin hallway connects all the rooms along the spine on two stories, and terminates in a generous double stairway. Clerestory windows provide natural light and ventilation, while a squared-off gable containing a rectangular window defines the stairway landing. A bridge connects the head of the stairs to the second-floor hallway.

Fischer Residence

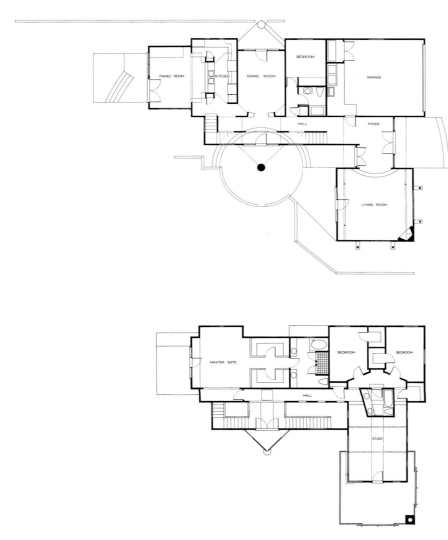

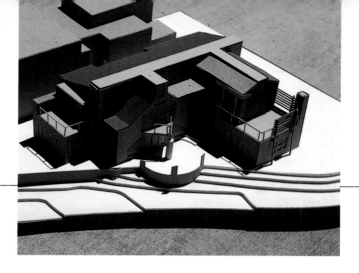

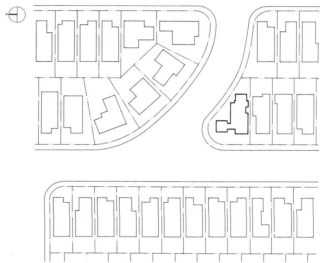

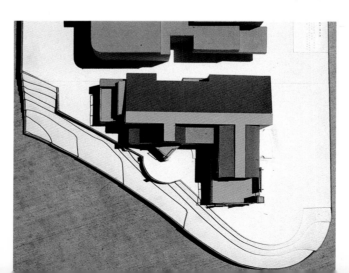

The Fischer Residence is sited on an irregularly shaped triangular lot, with the longest side of the triangle taken up by a spine of functional spaces: the family room, kitchen, dining room, and garage. The apex of the site is dominated by the square living room "pavilion".

Fischer Residence

Major interior public spaces of the house are signaled by external formal elements: The double stairway is marked on the exterior with a squared-off gabled element. A small triangular balcony opens from the second-floor foyer.

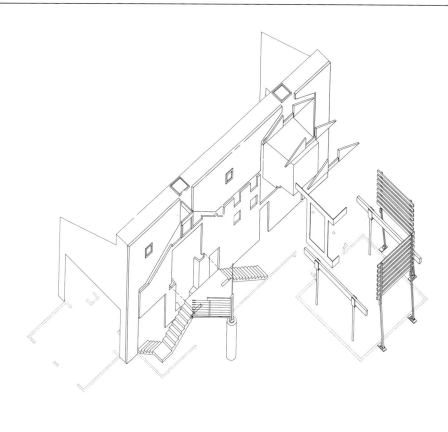

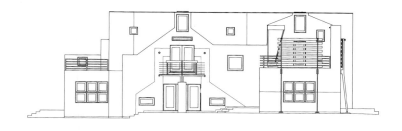

The apparent mass of the house is broken down into a series of smaller forms and articulated in a variety of materials, including concrete block, stucco, steel, and timber. The hallway is the main spatial experience of the house (opposite page). A mezzanine celebrates the arrival at the top of the double staircase, located at the terminus of the hallway.

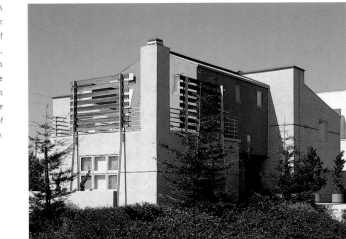

# Garner Residence

Located adjacent to the canals in Venice, California, this 2,800-square-foot house is sited to maximize use of a small corner lot. Binder designed an L-shaped plan that allows all building elements to embrace a landscaped entry courtyard. This "outdoor room" has both visual and physical access to the home, but remains cloistered from the two streets and alley that border three sides of the site.

The clients requested a "big house" program on a small urban site: a master suite and sitting room, a second bedroom, family room, study, separate dining room, breakfast nook, and three-car garage. In addition, the property fell under the jurisdiction of the California Coastal Commission. As a result, additional limitations were placed on the design of the single family residence, including required setbacks and a height restriction of 30 feet.

Public and private zones are separated on the two levels. The sitting area adjacent to the master bedroom is modeled as a separate pavilion; a large square window dominates the space. The result is a village-like, residential compound of simple volumes that provides an appropriate counterpoint to its densely developed neighborhood. Common building materials, including lap siding, stucco, steel, and concrete block, give the building a unique vocabulary within its urban context.

Garner Residence

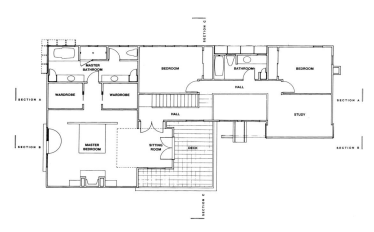

SECOND LEVEL

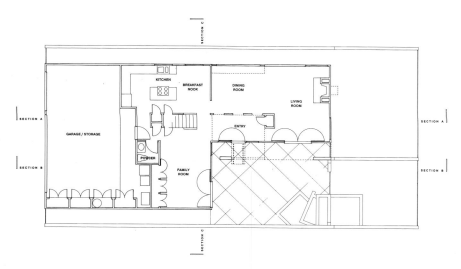

FIRST LEVEL

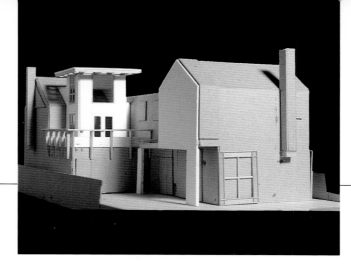

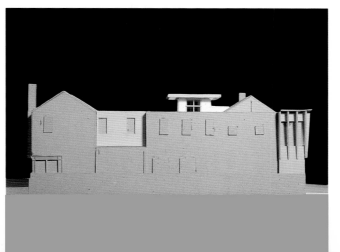

The L-shaped plan of the Garner Residence allows all building elements to embrace a private landscaped courtyard (opposite page).

0    25    50    100

Public and private zones are separated on two levels, with the connection occurring through circulation and volume at the core of the house. The second-floor sitting area—adjacent to the master bedroom—is modeled as a pavilion with large windows and a flat roof.

NORTHWEST ELEVATION

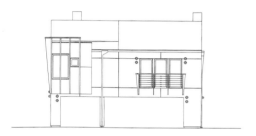

SECTION C

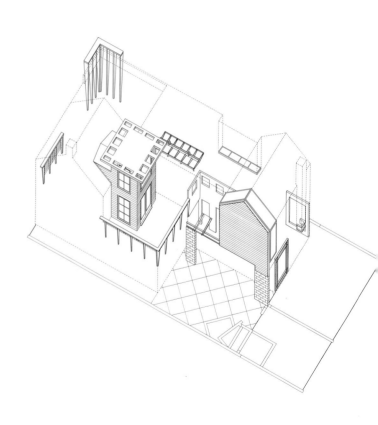

EAST ELEVATION

NORTHEAST ELEVATION

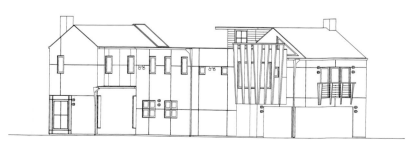

NORTH ELEVATION

# Stearns Residence

The renovation program for an undistinguished 1,600-square-foot, single-family residence called for 1,800 square feet of new space: three bedrooms, two bathrooms, a stair tower, and storage rooms. Binder devised a remodeling scheme that evolved from a series of new masonry forms overlaid on the existing artifact—a typical, single-story, suburban Ranch-style house. As an ordering device, the original building and the imposed new structural elements dictate spaces, define the circulation, and become furniture and objects both indoors and outdoors.

The new system of volumes, structures, and materials is first evident at the residence's entrance and reoccurs throughout the house. The new entry "bunker" reorients the house away from a busy front street to a quieter side street. By creating a new approach facade, the architect changes the reading of the scale of the site to take advantage of the expansive front yard setbacks. A large skylight crowns the foyer and mediates between the interior and exterior, giving each characteristics of the other.

The shape and scale of the original Ranch-style house set the tone of the evolving new structure. Simple rectangular spaces of modest size continue throughout the renovated plan, with one change in spatial conception: primary rooms are now open to one another and are defined by structural elements, rather than by walls.

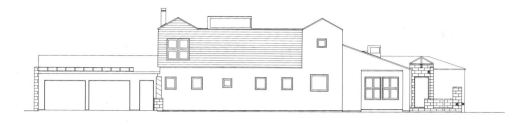

Stearns Residence

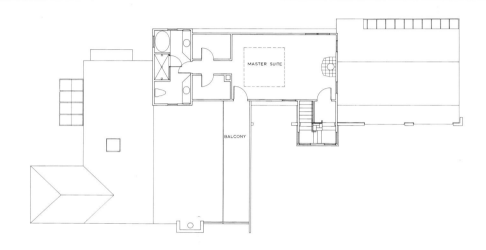

MASTER SUITE

BALCONY

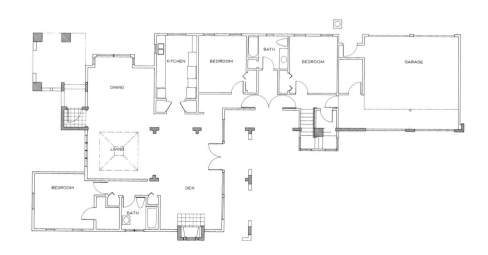

KITCHEN

BEDROOM

BATH

BEDROOM

GARAGE

DINING

LIVING

BEDROOM

DEN

BATH

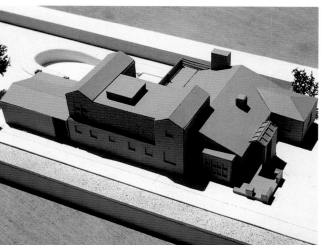

A major remodeling transformed a modest Ranch-style house into a 3,400-square-foot residence. Located on a long narrow corner lot, the renovated Stearns house is reoriented with a new formal approach on the longer side elevation, which faces east.

Interiors echo the simple and clear articulation of the exterior through straightforward, free-flowing spaces. Concrete block is repeated on the interior in a series of pillars and a fireplace. An entry skylight (middle and bottom) mediates outside and inside, giving each characteristics of the other.

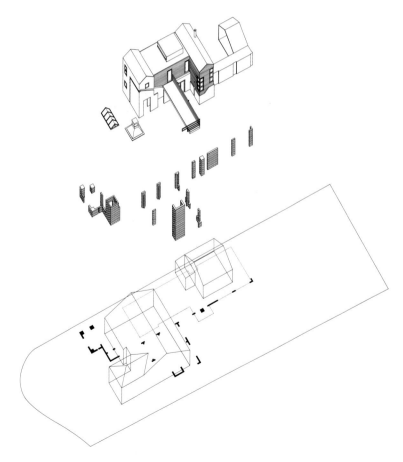

# Binder Residence

PLAYA DEL REY, CALIFORNIA

The components of this 2,800-square-foot house suggest a series of smaller units clustered around a central courtyard. This collection of tightly packed volumes surrounding an open space allows for almost no lot line setbacks on the side yards.

The building consists of three housing elements, which accommodate the garage, dining and kitchen, and living and bedrooms. The house also includes four prominent concrete block elements: an entry gate, a courtyard planter, the front door, and a fireplace stack. These masonry components assume a shifted plan grid juxtaposed with the orthogonal main housing elements. The courtyard wall reinforces the strength of the property line, while its patterning reflects the torqued grid on which the concrete pieces are sited: The vertical face of the garden wall features a graphic pattern that echoes this shifted grid. The architect further accentuated the composition with an interplay of materials; rich natural wood, patterned concrete block, painted steel and sheet metal, and stucco, all help to define the volumes.

Like a piazza, the courtyard defines the house. Sensitively scaled, open yet protected, it serves as the stage for the building's emerging personality.

Binder Residence

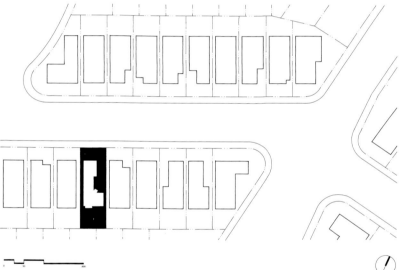

The parti of the Binder house is based on the notion of a courtyard surrounded by a series of various building elements. Along the rear of the site, a three-story stucco facade opens onto a small backyard garden.

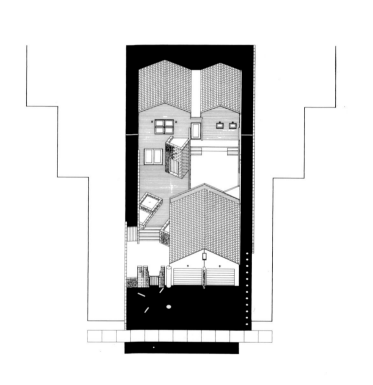

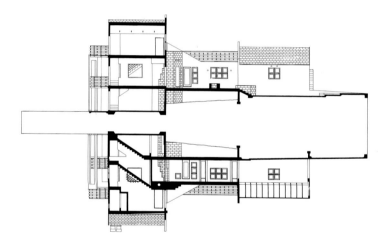

The design of the Binder Residence groups an assemblage of "rooms" around a courtyard, which eliminates lot line setback on the side yards. The building parts consist of three housing elements and four masonry elements.

# Bernstein Residence

SHERMAN OAKS, CALIFORNIA

Conceived as a "campus", the Bernstein project is a 1,750-square-foot addition to the original 850-square-foot 1940s home. The design acknowledges and retains the original structure while creating a distinct composition comprised of four new volumes. Binder draws from a palette of materials that is similar to that of the existing house, but reinterrupts the original board-and-batten and stucco in a very different manner and introduces concrete block.

Rather than a continuous building enveloping the existing structure, the addition is an assemblage of disparate components connected by a central circulation spine. This linear space is the unifying element of the house and connects the various new sections—a living room, den, three bedrooms, two bathrooms, and a breakfast room. The nature of this central spine changes throughout the house, culminating in a torqued stairway that recalls the irregular shape of the property.

To clarify the distinction between old and new, the architect employs a hierarchy of forms and volumes. The building's distinct roof line defines each of the four new components; exterior volumes become pure expressions of interior spaces. An entry portico crafted of wire glass mediates between the existing garage and a new living room pavilion crowned with a pyramidal roof. A curved wall of concrete block defines the tower element as a primary feature for the backyard. The two-story bedroom wing, with its gabled roof, assumes its own geometry and anchors the northern edge of the site.

The plan of the Bernstein Residence is organized around a central circulation spine that travels through the building, culminating in a torqued stairway that recalls the irregular configuration of the site. The disparate components of the house are defined by a variety of foundation "cradles" and rooflines. The vocabulary of exterior materials includes concrete block, stucco, and board-and-batten.

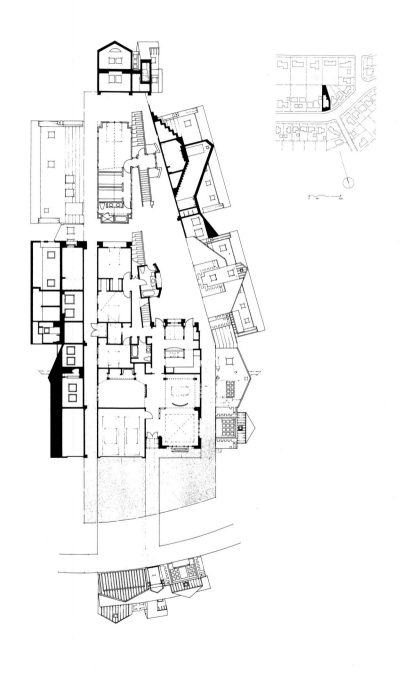

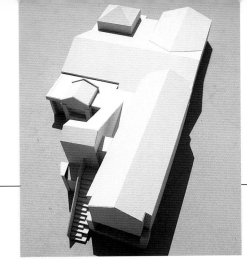

Bernstein Residence

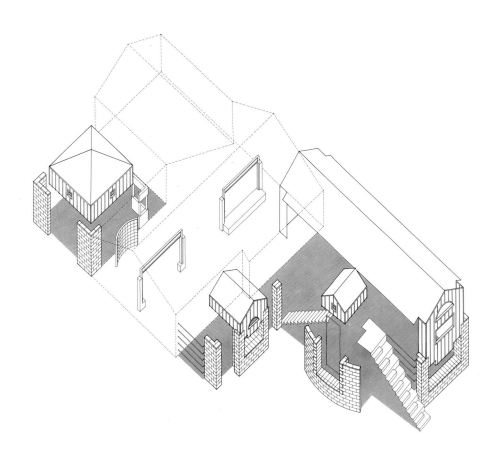

The interior spaces are mediated by
a new transverse column and frame
that supports the original ridge of the
existing house and defines the main
living spaces. A screen wall of curved
glass block delineates the dining room.

In Progress ▶

# Hesperia Fire Station #5

HESPERIA, CALIFORNIA

Located in the high desert of Southern California, this 9,000-square-foot fire station will house a triple-bay apparatus barn, dormitory space for 8 fire fighters (expandable to 15), a day room with kitchen, male and female lockers, a decontamination room, and administrative offices for duty chief and paramedics.

The program calls for horizontal hose drying racks rather than a hose-drying tower. Without a vertical element to provide the operative imagery, the fire station will hug the ground in a silhouette, reminiscent of a western fort built of concrete block. To deflect the desert winds, the scheme will incorporate a canopy of sheet metal supported by concrete block and steel structural members, which will extend across the front of the building like a marquee. Additional low walls at the entry will baffle the wind. The metal canopy and accent bands of contrasting split-face block will accentuate the overall horizontality of the structure.

The fire station's housing units will be clustered around an open-air private courtyard that contains a permanent, structural sun screen. The screen's canted roof is designed to provide a sheltered space for the fire fighters to use as an outdoor living room.

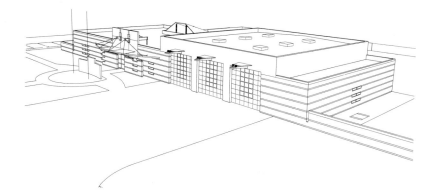

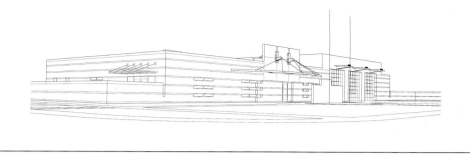

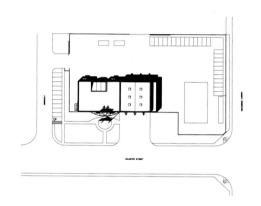

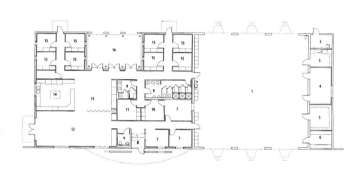

1. APPARATUS BAY
2. DECONTAMINATION ROOM
3. LAUNDRY ROOM
4. WORK ROOM
5. MAINTENANCE/EQUIPMENT
6. AIRPAK FILLING & STORAGE
7. OFFICE
8. RECEPTION
9. RESTROOM/SHOWER FACILITY
10. DUTY CAPTAIN ROOM
11. DUTY CHIEF ROOM
12. DAY ROOM/TRAINING
13. DINING AREA
14. KITCHEN
15. DORMITORY ROOM
16. OUTDOOR PATIO

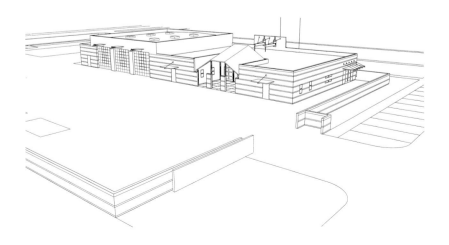

# Ackerman Student Union

UNIVERSITY OF CALIFORNIA, LOS ANGELES
LOS ANGELES, CALIFORNIA

This major expansion plan for UCLA's Ackerman Student Union Building will provide 40,000 square feet of new space on the first two levels and will redesign the original 1960s, five-story building, adding seismic, life safety, and accessibility upgrades. The program also calls for a collaborative urban design solution that will reconfigure both streetscape and scale along the adjacent Westwood Plaza and Bruin Walk, the campus's most public pedestrian zone.

The west and north facades will have a new, two-story base, designed to give the student union a heightened stature and legibility. These new elevations will be clad in a pattern of alternating dark red sandstone and cast-in-place integral color concrete. Horizontal bandings will change in a deliberately manipulated manner as they progress up the facade to reflect and punctuate the building's interior volumes and functions. Consistent with the urban design intentions of the campus, an entrance "pavilion" will anchor the northwest corner, and will house a second-floor reading room with an elevated volume. Inside, the double-height reading room will feature an articulated, folded-plywood ceiling and exposed sandstone and concrete walls.

The building's proposed new two-story base supports a 15,000-square-foot roof deck, planned to provide a generous open-air seating and dining area. The roof deck will be distinguished by arced trellises crafted of huge glu-lam beams supported by pre-cast concrete columns and steel tie-down rods. The roof forms of the main entrance pavilion, the northeast entry, and the stairtower are designed to further animate the scale of the roof deck and to read as "buildings" that border and define this outdoor urban space.

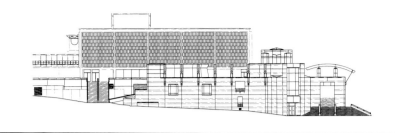

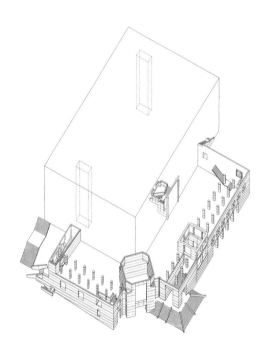

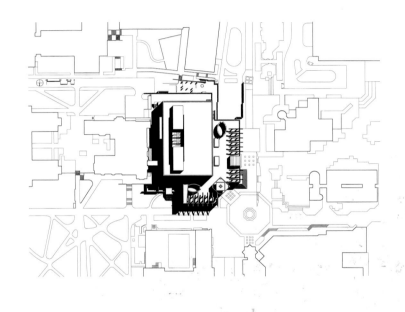

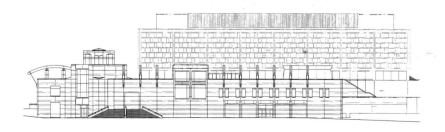

# Eagle Rock Elementary School

Providing space for a computer magnet program, this two-story school will be an autonomous structure composed of seven classrooms, cafeteria, lunch shelter, kitchen, storage, custodial space, and
restrooms. The new building is to be located on the campus of an existing elementary school built
around 1900 in a traditional mission style. For the new 16,000-square-foot facility, Binder used two
complementary colors of stucco and chose concrete block for its arcade. In deference to the original
school, the narrow pitch of the roof will be clad in red clay tiles.

The structure features a compact footprint to maximize the remaining school property for play
areas. The building, parking, and service areas are sited along a bordering parkway adjacent to and
aligned with the original school to optimize open space and views, and to allow for playground security.

The first floor will house a multi-purpose room/lunch room and support spaces; the second floor
will contain classrooms and teacher workrooms. For the second floor, the architect designed a hallway
that will include large, pop-up monitors and high, clerestory windows. Rooftop mechanical equipment
is set between the light monitors. This planned addition to the campus is intentionally contemporary
but designed to be compatible with the adjacent historical buildings.

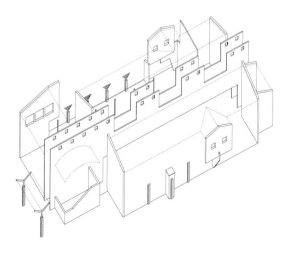

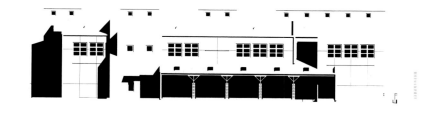

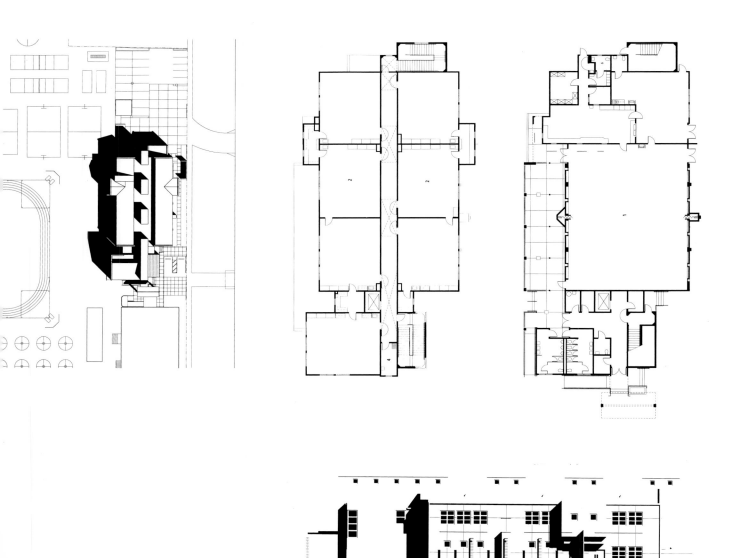

# Palmdale Airport Terminal

LOS ANGELES DEPARTMENT OF AIRPORTS
PALMDALE, CALIFORNIA

The desire to capture the drama of flight has repeatedly inspired architects to design memorable structures, such as Eero Saarinen's Dulles Airport. The design for the Palmdale International Airport will also evoke the adventure of air travel, with a small but expressive, 11,000-square-foot terminal building. The design for the airport terminal derives from the notion of three parallel geometric surfaces that will define curbside, entrance lobby, and baggage pick-up areas; ticketing and waiting spaces; and boarding and de-planing avenues. Each of these areas will allow independent expansion and flexibility. The volumes will alternate between a lower entry zone, a high bay, and a long span shed for ticketing and waiting. Continuous metal canopies supported by columns will provide shelter along the entry facades.

The flight apron will be full-size, accommodating three commercial jets. Exterior facades will feature a pattern of alternating smooth- and split-face concrete block. A large clerestory over the administrative offices will provide natural light, while patterns in the floor finishes and custom lighting fixtures will create a counterpoint to the strong orthogonal system of the structure.

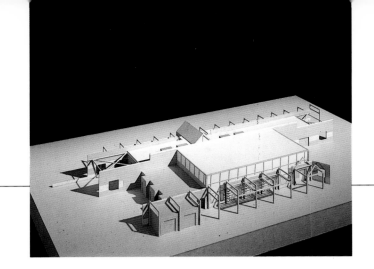

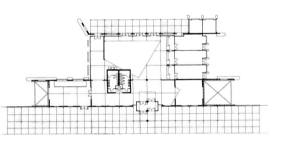

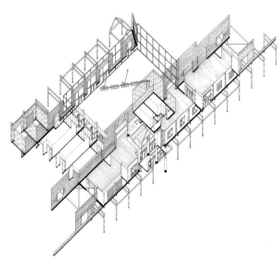

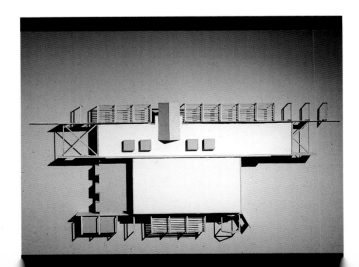

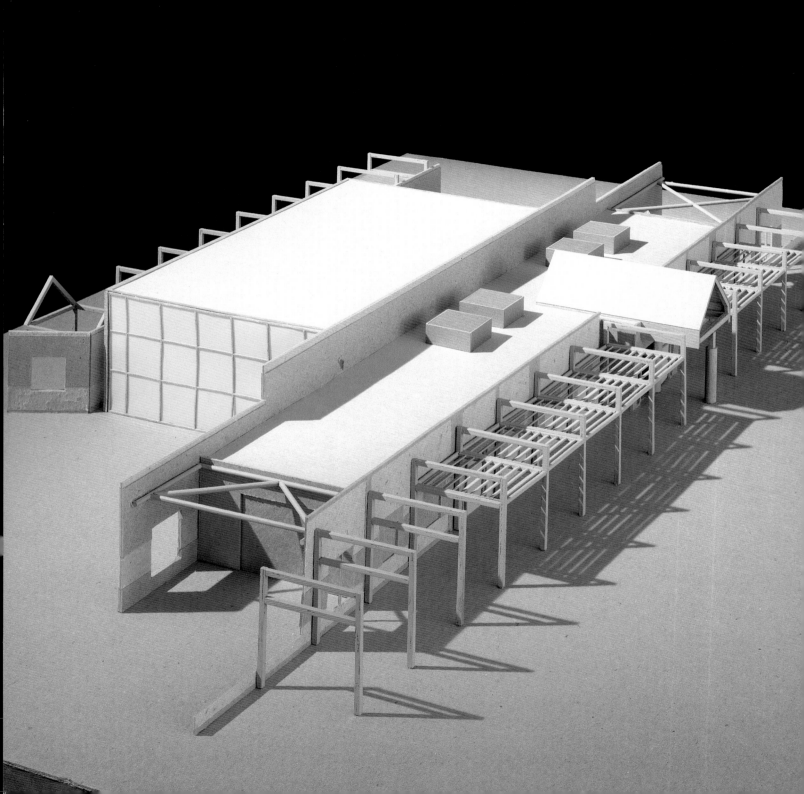

# Appendix ▶

# List of Works and Credits

**UNIVERSITY DINING COMPLEX**
CALIFORNIA POLYTECHNIC STATE UNIVERSITY, SAN LUIS OBISPO
1994, San Luis Obispo, California

Client: California State Polytechnic University Foundation, San Luis Obispo
Project Team: Rebecca L. Binder FAIA, Kim A. Walsh AIA, Tom Di Santo, Steve Lesko,
    Chilin Huang, Kevin Shibata
Structural Engineer: Brandow & Johnston Associates
Electrical Engineer: Mirahmadi & Associates
Mechanical Engineer: brice/downing/associates
Kitchen Consultant: Wattsco Design/Designers Food Facilities
Contractor: Shetler Construction Inc.
Photographer: © Jeff Goldberg/Esto
Model Photographer: David P. Bayles

**VISUAL ARTS FACILITY**
UNIVERSITY OF CALIFORNIA, SAN DIEGO
1993, La Jolla, California
Awards: AIA/San Diego Chapter, Design Award, 1990
    AIA/National Council, National Concrete Masonry Association, Award of
    Design Excellence, 1994
    AIA/California Council, Western States Concrete Masonry Association,
    Merit Award, 1994

Client: University of California, San Diego
Project Team: Rebecca L. Binder FAIA, Kim A. Walsh AIA, Ruth Hasell, Paul Harney,
    Kevin Shibata, Chilin Huang, Katie McMahon, Hao Hoang
Associate Architects: Neptune - Thomas - Davis
Structural Engineer: Burkett & Wong
Electrical Engineer: Randall-Lamb Associates
Mechanical Engineer: Merle Strum & Associates
Civil Engineer: Bement-Dainwood & Sturgeon
Landscape Architect: Kawasaki/Theilacker/Veno & Associates
Contractor: Ninteman Construction Company Inc.
Model: Dave Mobley
Model Photographer: David P. Bayles
Photographer: © Jeff Goldberg/Esto

**INFORMATION COMPUTER SCIENCES/ENGINEERING RESEARCH FACILITY**
**PHASE III** UNIVERSITY OF CALIFORNIA, IRVINE
1991, Irvine, California

Client: University of California, Irvine
Project Team: Rebecca L. Binder FAIA, Kim A. Walsh AIA, Paul Harney, Kevin Shibata,
    Hao Hoang, Brian Donnelly, Ruth Hasell
Structural Engineer: KPFF Consultants
Electrical Engineer: Mirahmadi & Associates
Mechanical Engineer: Tsuchiyama & Kaino
Civil Engineer: Arthur R. Leatores & Associates
Landscape Architect: Emmet L. Wemple & Associates
Contractor: A.R. Willinger Co., Inc.
Photographer: © Jeff Goldberg/Esto
Model Photographer: © Marvin Rand

**SOCIAL SCIENCES SATELLITE FOOD FACILITY**
UNIVERITY OF CALIFORNIA, IRVINE
1989, Irvine, California
Awards: AIA/California Council, Concrete Masonry Association of California and
    Nevada, Grand Design Award, 1990

Client: University of California, Irvine
Project Team: Rebecca L. Binder FAIA, Kim A. Walsh AIA, Joe Sion, Brian Donnelly
Associate Architects: Widom - Wein - Cohen
Structural Engineer: KPFF Consultants
Electrical Engineer: Mirahmadi & Associates
Mechanical Engineer: Stueven Associates
Landscape Architect: Emmet L. Wemple & Associates
Kitchen Consultant: Wattsco Design
Contractor: South Bay Construction
Photographers: David P. Bayles, © Marvin Rand (p.48, 54, 57)

**EATS RESTAURANT** 1985, El Segundo, California
Awards: AIA/Los Angeles Chapter, Merit Award, 1985
    AIA/California Council, Honor Award, 1985
    Restaurant & Hotel Magazine Design Award, Award of Merit, 1984

Client: Diane Thomson/George Mkitarian
Project Team: Rebecca L. Binder FAIA
Associate: James G. Stafford
Structural Engineer: Gordon Polon
Contractor: Alexander Construction
Photographer: © Marvin Rand

**PACIFIC TOWNHOUSES** 1982, Santa Monica, California
Awards: AIA/National Council, Honor Award, 1985
           AIA/California Council, Honor Award, 1985
           AIA/Los Angeles Chapter, Honor Award, 1982

Client: Gerald R. Fischer
Project Team: Rebecca L. Binder FAIA, Ron Fiala, Hao Hoang
Associate: James G. Stafford
Structural Engineer: George Kobayashi
Contractor: Fernandez Construction
Photographers: © Marvin Rand, David P. Bayles (p. 71 middle, bottom), Rebecca L.
      Binder (p. 68 middle)

**ARMACOST DUPLEX** 1989, Los Angeles, California

Client: Joe Bates & Mohammad Hamad
Project Team: Rebecca L. Binder FAIA, Kim A. Walsh AIA, Ruth Hasell, Jim Gelfat,
      Hao Hoang
Structural Engineer: Mohammad Namvar
Contractor: Frank Murphy Construction
Photographer: © Marvin Rand

**FISCHER RESIDENCE** 1987, Playa del Rey, California

Client: Gerald R. Fischer
Project Team: Rebecca L. Binder FAIA, Kim A. Walsh AIA, Joe Sion, Hao Hoang
Structural Engineer: Gordon Polon
Contractor: Fischer Construction
Photographers: David P. Bayles, © Alexander Vertikoff (p. 78, 86 middle, bottom,
      87)

**GARNER RESIDENCE** 1992, Venice, California

Client: Bill & Lucy Garner
Project Team: Rebecca L. Binder FAIA, Kim A. Walsh AIA, Joe Sion, Kevin Shibata,
      Ruth Hasell
Structural Engineer: Mohammad Namvar
Contractor: Frank Murphy Construction
Photographer: ©Jeff Goldberg/Esto, Scot Zimmerman (p. 93 top, p. 94)
Model Photographer: Joe Sion

**STEARNS RESIDENCE** 1988, Sherman Oaks, California

Client: Kandice Stroh & Neal Stearns
Project Team: Rebecca L. Binder FAIA, Kim A. Walsh AIA, Lawrence Brisley, Joe Sion,
      Joyce Freedman
Structural Engineer: Gordon Polon
Contractor: Ralph Herman Construction
Photographer: David P. Bayles

**BINDER RESIDENCE** 1986, Playa del Rey, California
Awards: AIA/California Council, Concrete Masonry Institute of California & Nevada,
      Honor Award, 1986

Client: Martin & Sarah Binder
Project Team: Rebecca L. Binder FAIA, Kim A. Walsh AIA, Joe Sion, Craig Dykers,
      Lawrence Brisley
Structural Engineer: George Kobayashi
Contractor: Ralph Herman Construction
Photographer: David P. Bayles

**BERNSTEIN RESIDENCE** 1985, Sherman Oaks, California
Awards: AIA/Los Angeles Chapter, Honor Award, 1986

Client: Fredrick & Kaye Bernstein
Project Team: Rebecca L. Binder FAIA, Kim A. Walsh AIA, Lawrence Brisley,
      Joyce Freedman
Structural Engineer: Gordon Polon
Contractor: Ralph Herman Construction
Photographers: Tim Street-Porter, © Marvin Rand (p. 115 top, middle)

**HESPERIA FIRE STATION #5** 1995, Hesperia, California

Client: City of Hesperia
Project Team: Rebecca L. Binder FAIA, Kim A. Walsh AIA, Chilin Huang, Ruth Hasell
Structural Engineer: Brandow & Johnston Associates
Electrical Engineer: Mirahmadi & Associates
Mechanical Engineer: Mel Bilow
Civil Engineer: Mollenhauer, Higashi & Moore Inc.
Landscape Architect: Peter Brandow

**ACKERMAN STUDENT UNION**
UNIVERSITY OF CALIFORNIA, LOS ANGELES
1996, Los Angeles, California

Client: ASUCLA
Project Team: Rebecca L. Binder FAIA, Kim A. Walsh AIA, Ruth Hasell, Chilin Huang,
      Joe Sion, Kevin Shibata, Tom Di Santo, Steve Lesko, Jean Chu
Structural Engineer: Brandow & Johnston Associates
Electrical Engineer: Cohen & Kanwar, Inc.
Mechanical Engineer: Store, Matakovich & Wolfberg
Civil Engineer: Mollenhauer, Higashi & Moore Inc.
Landscape Architect: Emmet L. Wemple & Associates
Contractor: Ray Wilson Construction


**EAGLE ROCK ELEMENTARY SCHOOL**
LOS ANGELES UNIFIED SCHOOL DISTRICT
1994, Eagle Rock, California

Client: Los Angeles Unified School District
Project Team: Rebecca L. Binder FAIA, Kim A. Walsh AIA, Ruth Hasell, Tom Di Santo,
      Joe Sion, Jim Gelfat, Scott Stapleton
Structural Engineer: Grossman & Speer Associates Inc.
Electrical Engineer: Pacific Engineers Group
Mechanical Engineer: Maroko & Associates
Civil Engineer: Arthur R. Leatores & Associates
Landscape Architect: Emmet L. Wemple & Associates
Contractor: Steed Brothers Construction Co.


**PALMDALE AIRPORT TERMINAL**
LOS ANGELES DEPARTMENT OF AIRPORTS
Palmdale, California

Client: Los Angeles Department of Airports
Project Team: Rebecca L. Binder FAIA, Kim A. Walsh AIA, Joe Sion, Lawrence Brisley,
      Paul Norris, Joyce Freedman
Executive Engineer: VTN
Model Photographer: David P. Bayles


Office Photo: © Tom Bonner

Clockwise from left: Will Chung, Rebecca Binder, Timothy Young, Kim Walsh, Joe Sion, Kevin Shibata, Chilin Huang, Gary Fischer, Ruth Hasell, Tom Di Santo (at the Binder residence)

# ACKNOWLEDGEMENTS

I would like to thank Stanley Tigerman for the *bon mots*; Lynn Nesmith, Connexus Visual Communication, AIA Press, and Rockport Publishers for their talent and efforts; our supportive clients for the opportunities they afforded us in design; our photographers for capturing these designs; our dedicated young architectural staff for their diligence; Gary for tirelessly watching the children and the computers;

and my partner Kim Walsh.

Dedication:

For
Genevieve and Maximilian
Sarah and Martin